The Empath and Shamanic Energy Work

ELAINE LA JOIE

DEDICATION

To Grant, my first guinea pig, look what happened!

CONTENTS

ACKNOWLEDGMENTS

I want to acknowledge my teachers, Debra Grace, Alberto Villoldo, Linda Fitch, Greta Holmes, Marv Harwood and Wake Wheeler. I feel blessed to have learned so much from you. I also thank all my clients for sharing their healing with me. This book wouldn't have been possible without all of you.

1 INTRODUCTION

I am an Empath who has been working as a coach, mentor, and shaman for about ten years. Most of my clients are also Empaths. I decided to write this book when I realized that I repeated the same concepts and materials to my clients, and those clients usually used their new knowledge for great improvement in their lives. Since Empaths tend to love books on self-improvement, writing one of my own seemed like the next right step, especially since not all Empaths have access to their own personal shaman. My teachers have included other Empaths, like Sonia Choquette and Julia Cameron, plus shaman teachers like Alberto Villoldo, Linda Fitch, Debra Grace, Greta Holmes, and Marv Harwood. If you've enjoyed Sonia Choquette's and Julia Cameron's work, you will most likely find this book useful. The shaman likes to get to the deep, nitty-gritty, and sometimes painfully messy work and release it. So, some of the work in this book may not feel inspirational or particularly easy to read. But, if you are an Empath, you probably aren't afraid of dealing with the darker emotional states, and in fact you may be relieved to hear how one Empath overcame obstacles particular to Empaths.

WHAT IS AN EMPATH?

One way of describing an Empath is the ability of someone to feel the emotional, mental, and physical symptoms of people around the Empath, especially those that the Empath loves, as if those emotions and sensations originated in the Empath. The untrained

1

Empath literally cannot tell the difference between her emotions, thoughts, and physical sensations and those of another. An Empath can easily absorb the emotions of others, and in some cases, she can be overtaken by the physical symptoms of others. Without skill, the Empath can become very ill. Some Empaths are so sensitive that they cannot take public transportation and must avoid large groups of people or feel completely overwhelmed by what most people consider normal stimuli.

Empaths who work with me learn how to manage their Empathy so they can be at choice about how much they want to open to others. They learn how to Observe, not Absorb, as my teacher Sonia Choquette says. They also learn techniques to shake off excess energy and how to protect themselves during overwhelming situations.

Honoring the Empath's sensitivity is the first step in healing. This very sensitivity is the reason that Empaths make natural healers, artists, and intuitives. Empaths can also make great performers, literally channeling their roles. It is this ability to role-play and to respond that can get Empaths into trouble in their relationships; Empaths can confuse a performance or a role with their essential selves.

In such cases Empaths can use their sensitivity to collude with the group instead of honor their individuality. The Empath can be easily caught up in drama because she is so psychically in tune with everyone around her. The ability of the Empath to enmesh herself with others can lead the Empath to waste her life supporting others without her understanding how she became the anchor for their emotional support.

THE MYTHIC REALITY: ARCHETYPES

My discussion of the Empath, especially within relationships, hinges on understanding the archetypal nature of the human experience. Archetypes are forces that are common to all human beings—they are part of the collective consciousness. The Empath can be described as an archetype. When we understand ourselves as archetype, we can understand our behavior in a less personalized way. Knowing the other archetypes with which Empaths tend to interact also helps us understand our relationships and how those predictably will unfold. In this book I'll discuss several archetypes that have been described in detail through the Enneagram, although no previous knowledge of the Enneagram is necessary.

For those of you unfamiliar with the Enneagram, it describes the motivations of nine major Archetypes. I like using the Enneagram rather than other personality type systems because the Enneagram focuses on belief systems and motivation rather than on behavior. In shamanic work, as we will see later, we create our world through the lens of our beliefs. If we can gain insight into our hidden belief system, we can create more effectively lives that we love and enjoy. The Enneagram, as described by Riso and Hudson, also touches on the levels of mental and emotional health of each of the archetypes, and on what happens to each archetype as we become more aware of our motivations. The Classic Empath is most closely related to the Four on the Enneagram.

THE MYTHIC REALITY: SHAMANIC WORK AND THE SACRED

I will use examples from my life and my clients', including discussion of shamanic energy work as I proceed. Some shamanic knowledge has similar concepts as psychology, such as the Drama Triangle and the discussion on projection. However, I am a shaman, so those readers with a psychology background may notice differences in descriptions. The shaman works at the level of the Soul's Journey, where Myth and Archetype (the experience of the Collective) reside. As my teacher, Alberto Villoldo describes, we can think of reality as composed of four basic levels: the Literal level (physical body, what we could see, feel, and touch), the Symbolic level (emotional and mental mind), the Mythic level (soul's journey, archetypes, and the Sacred), and the Energetic level (energetic cords, subtle vibrations).

Teaching my clients to move into the Sacred, or the Mythic level can bring lasting change for many Empaths, who tend to create problems for themselves on the Emotional level. If you are reading this book, you probably are an Empath that hasn't had much success solving problems at the Symbolic level (mental mind and emotions); you might have become sick at the Literal level (the physical body) with various chronic physical ailments. Stepping into the Mythic plane and understanding archetypal forces may help ease suffering that in many cases is unnecessary.

When we step into the Mythic realm, we are stepping into an overview of the situation at hand. From the Mythic level we discover that archetypal forces run more of our literal lives than we realize. This also means that by understanding the archetypal nature of relationships, we can apply knowledge of the archetypes, especially those on the Drama Triangle, to many situations at the Literal and Symbolic levels of our lives.

On the Literal level nothing much may look amiss when a friend who is only five years younger than us tells us he thinks of us as he Big Sis. On the Symbolic level as Empaths we may get a weird vibe but reason with ourselves that we should feel honored to be thought of as Family. But by looking from the Mythic level we may see that our friend is trapped in the Victim Role as the Improperly Mothered Child and is projecting his old wounds onto us—we feel weird because we are expected to Mother him—we've been placed in the Role of Rescuer because his power to feel good about himself has been given over to us, and we may not be interested in playing that role. At the Energetic level we may see cords from our friend to us that pinch, bind and even drain us of our energy.

At the Mythic level, we can learn that most of Life is not personal (and Empaths tend to take everything personally.) Knowing that not much is personal can give us freedom to choose to engage or not to engage a relationship or a situation and therefore make it personal to us. If we understand our Enneagram type, including the blind spots of the typical Empath, we can look at how the archetype is running us at the Symbolic level (our emotions and thoughts) and at the Literal level (physical illness or even weight gain). Suddenly Life can become less confusing and more about changing habits and behavior rather than feeling stuck and confused. We can keep the gifts of our Enneagram Archetype and be wary of the deeper blind spots. Life becomes a practice of self-mastery instead of simply unconsciously living out a few archetypal forces.

In modern Western Society, we have left much of the honoring of the Mythic experience behind. The Mythic level is not only the place of the archetypes, but it is also the realm of the Soul or the Heart. When we leave this reality out of our lives, Empaths tend to become disconnected from our hearts and stuck in the

Emotional/Mental realm. If problems arise at the Emotional/Mental realm, then Empaths can become physically ill as well as we try to process this heavy energy through the physical body. When the Empath learns how to live consciously from the Mythic level, problems at the Emotional plane can be solved at the Mythic plane instead of processed at the Physical plane. Since the Mythic plane of consciousness does not have a "mental mind" it can be hard for us Westerners to figure out how it works enough to trust that it does work. If we don't know how it works, we might tend to dismiss it as silly. Instead of trying to figure out the Mythic realm, in this book I'll go straight to my personal experience and those of my clients to show the changes that can happen when we treat our entire life as Sacred by living from the Mythic level. When we can see our lives from the universal instead of the personal, the Empath suddenly has more choice and more freedom.

Once we become comfortable living our lives from the Mythic Realm, we can clean up old wounds and the unhappy beliefs that arose from those wounds. The shaman addresses problems rooted at both the Energetic and the Mythic planes. For many of my clients once the root problem is cleared at the Energetic and Mythic, they can move into what they want to create in their lives instead of living out the same relationship pattern or remaining blocked in their creativity. I'll cover different examples of shamanic energy work, including Soul Retrieval, Extractions, and Underworld Work and how once my clients are able to change their hidden belief system, they are able to change their lives.

When the wounds that led to the faulty beliefs are cleared, we are free to embark on a life of creativity and discovery. We are free to explore the gifts of the Empath: the ability to form deep connections and to enjoy extraordinary creativity. In turn, the Empath brings gifts to the rest of humanity in the form of healthy relationships, supportive community, and inspiring works of art.

In my work with clients, we always cover the Archetypal Drama Triangle of Disempowerment if they are having trouble in their relationships. (This book assumes the reader is familiar with all the concepts introduced in the first eBook, The Empath and the Archetypal Drama Triangle.) However, there are other deeper binds that can block a client's healing, or that can lead them to take a position on the Triangle. Most of these need the assistance of the shaman on the Mythic and Energetic planes to remove these binds, meaning that they are very hard to move from the Symbolic and the Literal levels without assistance. In this book I describe common blocks I have helped clients remove within the shamanic work session, but for those readers not familiar with shamanic energy work, I'll describe first tools and processes. For more descriptions of energy work and case studies, please visit my website.

2 THE MYTHIC LEVEL

WORKING AT THE MYTHIC LEVEL IS BEYOND THE LOGICAL AND ANALYTICAL MIND

Although my clients come to me to tell me their Story and we do discuss issues, the most important work with me is done on the Energetic and Mythic levels, not at the level of the Symbolic or the Mental Mind. Most of the people who come to see me have done lots of personal work and workshops in healing themselves, and while they have made progress, usually those deeper core issues don't move much or they do but later return full blown. Why? What has happened?

Many of these issues are rooted at the Energetic and Mythic levels, where there are no words. At the Mythic there are only images, and at the Energetic, there is just the blueprint energy of the client. So, if my client spends his time talking about a problem that is not rooted at the level of Mind, that problem is very unlikely to shift unless he has an ah ha moment at a Heart level (the Mythic Level). By Heart I mean that inner part of us that knows our own personal truths no matter what our circumstances or our emotional and mental state. Instead of waiting for that insightful heart-based moment of grace, I have clients access the Mythic level directly by using ceremony and sandpainting, and as the Shaman I intervene at the Energetic level. By working at these two levels, major healing breakthroughs can happen.

Sometimes these breakthroughs are miraculous—so miraculous that the client completely forgets she ever had a problem. However, many times there's still the hard work ahead of bringing those changes at the Energetic and Mythic levels down to the Emotional and Physical levels. We are creatures of the Mind; we want to understand what is happening as we shift. Sometimes our systems can handle only so much at a time, and the work happens in layers as the emotions and the physical body adjust to these changes. I've worked with many a client who had layer after layer of wounds and hurts come off in a steady but years-long journey as the psyche went through the painful process of acknowledging pain and of understanding their family system, especially when emotional and physical abuse was involved. Those people would not have been able to absorb it all at once.

Working at the Mythic and Energetic levels, and then turning the outcome over to Spirit allows for the best healing of the client, according to what the client's Soul and the Great Spirit knows she needs at the time. Turning the outcome over to Spirit means a certain detachment to how the process will unfold. This can be frustrating for clients in wanting one of the miraculous cures. I have watched clients who have gone through tremendous change think that not much has happened. However, when they go home to visit their family after a long time away, people around them comment on the change that was obvious to me but not to them. I had one client's brother ask her if she was taking medication because she seemed so much happier and well adjusted. The major difference in her life was significant shamanic work combined with her actively doing her assigned homework at the Mythic level.

In my own healing process, especially in the last few years, I have given up daily journaling about my own personal healing sessions, because I know my mind cannot make sense of them at the time, but it will figure it out later if it's important enough to remember. One of my teachers spent a year mentoring me through a huge transition in my life around stepping into power. He asked if I would write myself up as a case study for him, however the changes were so complete, that I literally could not remember what my problems had been. I knew I had had them and they had been holding me back, but because the healing was so deep, I couldn't remember what I had identified with as the problem. This is the magic of working at the Mythic with a shaman.

SHAMANIC TOOLS DURING A SESSION AND MYTHIC HOMEWORK

Many of the stories in this book include descriptions of some of the soul retrievals and other energy work performed during sessions so that my clients could heal the wound that led to the faulty belief that caused the unhappy pattern. I want to describe briefly what a session is like so that the reader is not confused by unfamiliar tools. As a shaman I work with many tools from nature. One of my most important tools is my shaman's altar, or my mesa. My mesa has several stones in it that have become allies by helping me with my own personal work. While it may seem odd to make a stone into an ally (it certainly did to me when I first began this work) my stones have a lot to say about my clients. When clients pick a particular stone to work with, their choice tells me much about the issue at hand, as well as where the client is in the process of healing it. The client informs the stone by blowing the issue into it. Remember, the shaman works at the Mythic and Energetic Levels, so what represents the issue (in this case, the breath) is actually the issue.

I then take the stone and see where the information is stored in the client's energy body. Our bodies have seven major centers called chakras that connect all four levels of reality (physical, mental/emotional, mythic, and energetic). See Sonia Choquette's True Balance for a good introduction to the chakras. Each chakra is responsible for different states of consciousness. By holding the stone over each of the chakras I can sense where the stuck energy is lodged. In a session, I do a clearing process (called Illumination or Yanachaqui) of the affected chakras before journeying to the underworld to clean up the wounds and retrieve soul parts.

Sometimes this energy is stuck enough that I need the assistance of other tools such as extraction crystals, usually made out of clear quartz, to move the energy out of the chakra. I'll also use Florida Water (alcohol and flower essences) and sage and palo santo smoke to move heavy energy off the chakras and the energy body. Usually Empath clients can feel the energy move, even though most of my sessions are done over the phone. While this may seem physically impossible, we must remember that this is energy work: it is done on the energetic plane, not the physical plane. The energetic plane is outside space-time—it is non-local. And, even though we may be moving out significant trauma, the client usually does not feel emotional or have a cathartic response, precisely because the work is done at the deeper energetic, not the emotional/mental level.

Once the actual energy work part of the session is completed, then we move on to the Mythic work, which includes using tools such as sandpaintings and altars. I bring back to the client a soul's journey story (or a mythic map as Alberto Villoldo calls it), and the client works with that story as she integrates her soul part. For homework the client builds an altar or a sandpainting (sometimes both) as a way of honoring the parts that have come back and honoring the parts that need releasing in order to move forward. I have my clients make sandpaintings (done usually outdoors or in a plastic container filled with soil or sand) to release energy that their system cannot process down to the mother earth instead. The altar, usually made in a special spot like a small table or a shelf, honors the soul parts that have returned and serves as a container for the new energy that has been returned, or that the client wants to build. This altar remains up for at least two weeks as the energy work shifts down into the Mythic Level. If my client has emotional responses to the work, she can blow those emotions into the altar so it will process at the Mythic Level instead of at the Emotional/Mental level.

All Empaths can relate to getting the psychic flu, in which some emotional upset has gotten away from us so that we become ill, but we know it's stuck emotional stuff. Many of these psychic flus can be avoided by putting them into an altar or sandpainting and letting them process on the Mythic instead of on the Physical level. This one task of working with altars or sandpaintings, although many of my clients resist doing it, is an essential tool in making the shamanic session really stick. Once again, one need not have an energy work session to use a sandpainting or altar. If something is not going as well as we would like for ourselves, we can put it into a sandpainting and let the issue process on the Mythic Level instead of trying to force a solution on the mental/emotional plane. We can avoid a psychic flu by using the altar or sandpainting to process at the Mythic level rather than become emotionally over wrought or physically ill.

Another great use of sandpainting for Empaths is the tendency for us to pick up the emotions and thoughts of people around us. Putting those foreign emotions and thoughts into a sandpainting along with a shot glass of Epsom salts to absorb the foreign energy can clear our system. Altars can be built for protection of our family and our home as well. If we feel like we are under psychic attack from a friend or relative, we can hide ourselves energetically by using a sandpainting or altar. I do this as a general protection by encircling a representation of myself within a protective layer of kosher salt in an altar. I have also protected myself with using a sandpainting when under direct psychic attack—building the sandpainting directly on the earth helps to drain the energy of that negative relationship directly into the earth.

While sandpainting and altars can seem like a silly tool to the mental mind, I cannot emphasize how important these Mythic tools are in integrating the shamanic energy work. Many times I will have a client call or email me with emotional upset after a soul retrieval. Usually they have not done their sandpaintings. Once they complete the sandpainting, the emotions settle. Even ten years later I sometimes am startled by the effectiveness of doing sandpainting. Recently I had built a sandpainting because some old issues had been aggravating me. I came out the next day to look at the sandpainting, still feeling upset. Just by moving a few rocks and twigs to different locations within the painting, I immediately felt better. While this sort of blatantly obvious shift isn't guaranteed to happen, it is essential to do this homework anyway and trust that at the Mythic Level something is shifting.

Building up a friendly relationship to fire, or fire ceremony, when used at the Mythic level, becomes a tool for fast transformation. If a client has something that is really stuck that needs to be released, I usually have him put the issue in a sandpainting but blow it into a stick instead of a stone or other noncombustible. Then after the issue has simmered in the painting for a day or two, I have him do a ceremonial fire and burn the stick at the fire. How the stick burns in the fire tells how the issue has shifted. If it burns quickly and completely to ash, the issue is most likely resolved. If it half burns, we can guess that there is more work to do. If it refuses to burn, that sometimes indicates that my client is hanging on to the issue and we need to do more exploration on why he does not want to let go.

The actual fire ceremony can be as simple as burning a small piece of paper in a candle flame and saying a prayer, or as complex as a bonfire, feeding it with olive oil, and taking twigs and other offerings to the fire. Most of my clients do a simple alcohol and Epsom salt fire in a disposable potpie tin outdoors, using toothpicks as offerings. The important point is that this is not a just a fire at the literal level but a sacred fire where we ask fire to become our friend and help us with our transformation.

These mythic tools are particularly helpful for Empaths, since we tend to do our processing at the emotional/mental and physical levels. Moving issues up to the Mythic gives us another way of processing that doesn't have so much suffering in it. The work is still hard, but at the same time becomes easier. Plus, since the work is outside of the mental mind, we can give ourselves a break and go do something fun while the sandpaintings and altars are cooking. In other words, we're removing much of the suffering, emotional and physical, from the healing process.

The following are difficult situations that can be helped in shamanic sessions.

3 THE PSYCHE, THE UNDERWORLD, AND SOUL RETRIEVAL

The Shaman looks at the human psyche as a realm that can be visited. When a client has suffered a wound, or a pattern emerges in her life that leads to unhappy outcomes, as a shaman, I immediately suspect I will need to go and take a look around part of the client's psyche called the Underworld. From the shaman's perspective the Underworld houses our subconscious mind as well as the collective unconscious mind and some of the archetypal forces. (As an example, I've had several clients stuck with a samurai warrior archetype. These clients lived out the code of the warrior even though such a code no longer applied in modern society. They also had samurai décor in their homes, watched Japanese movies, and one client had started Kendo classes.) Family stories are found here as well. Sometimes a client's pattern was rooted in a wound and a belief system created by an ancestor. Sometimes the pattern appears as if it originated as a past life. Whether one believes literally in past lives or not is irrelevant. What is important is how the Story and the beliefs that go along with it are manifesting in the client's life in the present.

The shaman journeys to the client's underworld, looks for the Story of what caused the belief that is manifesting the client's unhappy outcome in the present, heals the wounds that led to the faulty belief, removes the faulty belief in order to make room for a new, more helpful belief, retrieves any lost bits of consciousness that broke away because they could not handle what was happening, and returns these to the client. These lost bits of consciousness are called

Soul Parts. Only unwounded Soul Parts are returned. These Soul Parts broke away so they would not be injured by what happened when the original wound occurred. On top of this, the client has considerable personal work to do outside the session to break any habits that arose from the wound and the faulty beliefs so the soul part will stay and reintegrate.

The way such soul loss manifests in the client's life depends on the severity of the wound. Sometimes the client feels like he was never the same or never fully recovers from grief or shock. Sometimes emotional dissociation in some situations or being unable to fully feel in general indicates soul loss. In severe cases there might be gaps in memory or splits in personality. When wounds aren't literally severe, the client may still have taken them as severe at the Symbolic (Emotional and Mental level). I've dealt with several Empaths who were terrified of the dark as children and suffered huge soul loss, which led in turn to trust and creativity issues. Empaths who have been lost in the grocery store, bullied on the playground, or even watched their parents fight can suffer significant soul loss whereas others with less sensitive nervous systems might not.

Once a client experiences a soul retrieval and does the Mythic work of reintegrating that part of their consciousness, huge shifts in behavior and the ceasing of the pattern in the external world can occur. This can be done without having to talk much about the literal problem that first occurred, which can be an advantage for Empaths, since we tend to focus on the negative and on our wounds. At the same time, room must be made for the returning soul part, or else it is likely to leave again. If a client comes to me, wants to change her life, but is unwilling to make the changes necessary to accommodate the soul part, there is no point in negotiating with the soul part to return; the soul part will leave again and will be harder to convince to come back a second time.

I had a client who was incredibly gifted musically, and who couldn't help himself but to compose, to sing, to learn every instrument, and even to build some of his own. He was raised in a family where a steady job and income were considered more important and more practical than a musical career. Would music pay the bills? Would he be successful? His parents weren't sure, and thought a career in science or engineering would be a wiser choice. My client, having a Sensitive Scientist side, (see Motivations of the

Empath eBook for a fuller description of the Sensitive Scientist) had potential to be a technical person as well as an artist. While it was obvious to everyone else around him that he was incredibly gifted and could make a career of music, his energy was divided between science and music. This led him to tinkering at both instead of whole-heartedly committing to one, but neither made him money or gave him success, which irritated his wife.

On the physical level, this client suffered from sleep paralysis that had started after a nightmare and sleepwalking experience in puberty. Since that incident, every once in a while he would literally not be able to wake himself up, or parts of his body would go numb. He would also emotionally dissociate. The emotional dissociation indicated to me that he had suffered a significant soul loss during puberty, a time when our emotional state is so susceptible as the person goes through so much physical change.

Coincidentally, when we scheduled his session, he was just about to go on a road trip to honor his father, who had passed away years before. That explained to me why his father seemed to be hanging around in the background during our session. When I asked how he had died, my client told me the story of how his father had burst into his room late one evening to tell him to stop with his music; his father was trying to sleep. And at that point, my client told his father that he wanted to pursue music, he wanted music to be his living. His father left the room not feeling well, had a stroke a few hours later, and died a few days after that. This tragedy set up a significant subconscious belief that pursuing music led to the death of loved ones, putting my client in a double bind.

Not only did it feel on a deep emotional level like he had caused his father's death, he didn't have that most creative part of him (lost at puberty) available to pursue his music. In our sessions together, we did what is called death rites, and honored his father. As the shaman I made sure that his father crossed over successfully (he had been visiting relatives for years). The reason he hadn't crossed over was he hadn't been ready to die, and so much business had been left unfinished. My client, during the death rites session, had a chance to say goodbyes, and to also tell his father how everyone was doing, how everyone had moved on and that it was okay for his father to move on, too. As my client let his father go, my client could also move on.

Later we did a soul retrieval session to clear up the traumatic incident during adolescence. And with that, the sleep paralysis symptoms also cleared. Many Empaths are vulnerable during the night, especially as children, and especially when emotionally upset. Luckily, tools like soul retrieval exist to help heal the problem that originated years before. Soon after these two sessions my client moved seriously into a musical career. I reminded him that he needed to make room in his life for his creativity, which requires a lot of down time, unproductive time, and is not a linear practice. If he didn't do those things, the soul part might leave again.

My client wasn't able to make the room in his life, mainly because his life was packed full of other obligations. On top of this his wife, who was a Get-Things-Done Enneagram Type Eight, did not understand the creative process. While she loved and supported his dream, she wanted results, and she wanted to see a plan. Most of us who are Empaths and successfully creative know that there is no plan. Creativity is a process, and unpredictable at that—Spirit co-creates with us, and we cannot know the how of how it will work out, we only must show up. My client, feeling the pressure to please his wife and his wife's view of how his new career should unfold combined with their family life, could literally not make time for his music in a way that pleased her. Eventually the sleep paralysis returned, and the old status quo reinstated itself.

This is the risk of doing Soul Retrieval work. It requires that we make room for the new life that wants to come in with the returned soul part. My client was born to be a musician, but his adult life had been set up to be a part time science instructor and house husband. His family structure and his marriage were not flexible enough to accommodate the new soul part that came back that wanted space and creativity time. Now, this soul part will not come back a second time unless my client changes the structure first. Soul retrieval can be incredibly powerful work, but it usually requires a deep lifestyle change as well.

4 OPPORTUNISTIC ENTITIES

If you've read my stories on my website about Extractions, you probably already know that sometimes when a loved one dies, that person's consciousness can become confused and then attach to a person still living instead of moving on to the Upper World. (The Bardo, Heaven, etc.) That person can then take on the traits of the loved one, sometimes even becoming ill with the same symptoms if the person who died was sick. As a shaman I can "extract" the loved one and cross the person over to the other side, escorting him or her through the Bardo and all the way up to the Fourth Realm of individuated souls (Heaven).

In other cases we can take on a thought form of a loved one that gains so much energy it acts like an entity. An example of this would be a critical parent constantly chattering at us in the background. Such thought forms can be extracted in the same way as a person that has lost his way after death but these thought forms aren't really entities.

However, there are other Entities that are not so benign. These Opportunistic Entities are looking to take advantage of people in bodies to get an energetic feeding. They usually don't want to go through the hassle of making a body of their own, so they attach to someone in a body instead and cause trouble. The easiest target for these Opportunistic Entities is an emotionally distressed Empath or psychic child.

The Empathic or highly sensitive child in an extended moment of fear or stress psychically cries out for comfort or help. If no caregiver answers or responds in a way that makes the child feel safe and cared for, the Entity has an opportunity to answer instead. The child and the Entity make a deal or an agreement—a sense of safety and a feeling of at least not being completely abandoned in exchange for feeding the Entity. Usually a soul loss takes place for the child as well, making the child more vulnerable. In any case the child and the Entity exist in a sort of symbiotic relationship.

How do you know if your child has unintentionally made this deal with an Entity? Sometimes children develop unusual behaviors or become unreasonably clinging or afraid. Some children develop behaviors that look like OCD or they become extremely anxious. Some become people pleasers. Some become violent and mean for no apparent cause. In fact, it can be hard to tell just from behavior if your child has an entity. But if they suddenly begin acting out of character and they have also been put in a situation where they were anxious, afraid, or believed themselves to be in danger or abandoned, it is reasonable to have a shaman check them for an Entity and most definitely for Soul Loss.

While I've worked with several children with Entities attached or near by them, more commonly I pull Opportunistic Entities out of adult Empaths. All these Empaths made the agreement with the Entity when they were children and when they were extremely afraid or under extreme stress. In one case, a client was extremely afraid of the dark when sleeping in a strange house and accidentally called one in. In another case an Entity deliberately frightened the child and then the child called out for help and the Entity "rescued" him. This child lost his zest for life and became painfully self-conscious. In yet another case a client who had grown up in a chaotic household filled with arguments and physical violence had more than one Entity attached as an adult. Years later, when this client was in a funk, these Entities tried to taunt him into committing suicide.

As you can see, Opportunistic Entities are troublemakers. They feed off fear, anxiety, and anger. The more they stir up these emotions in the Empath the bigger feeding they get. They co-opt the Empath's power for their own, and they sabotage the Empath when she tries to step back into power. They love causing trouble not just to the Empath but also to the people around the Empath. Many times the Empath doesn't suspect she has an attachment to an Opportunistic Entity until she starts doing healing work or deep personal work. As she changes, the presence of the Entity becomes more obvious and less hidden. So, what does the adult Empath do next?

The most essential step for the Empath is to break the deal with the Entity. The Empath must look at what benefit she gets from the Entity now that she is an adult. Instead of safety and comfort that she might have missed from her parents as a child, as an adult the contract may have shifted into something different. Many Empaths live from a Victim Stance. The Victim Stance has the benefit of never having to take responsibility for ourselves. The Victim wants others to take care of her. The Victim wants life to be easy without putting in the work on the physical plane. In a way, living from a Victim Stance has considerable benefits. However, having a Victim Stance means that the Empath cannot get out of the contract with the Entity.

If we give up our Victim Stance, which means taking responsibility for our life as it is right now, reframing how we look at our life with the phrase, "I created this mess, what am I going to do to clean it up," no matter that we inadvertently created it as children, and taking small actions to clean up our lives, we step into power and into choice. Opportunistic Entities don't like that. They like us in our Victim Stance because we are helpless, hopeless, blaming others and circumstances for our lives, and powerless. All that beautiful creative power is up for grabs, and they will grab it.

Opportunistic Entities sabotage the healing work. I've had Empaths realize that they have an Opportunistic Entity, schedule a session to do the work to remove it, and fall asleep before the call. I've had Empaths completely forget conversations and directions that would lead to ejecting the Entity. I've had Empaths attack me personally for suggesting that their attachment to a Victim Stance was leaving the door open to the Opportunistic Entity while sounding nothing like their true selves. The Entity doesn't want to give up the attachment, and sometimes the Empath doesn't want to give it up, either. That is a valid choice. We don't have to break the deal with the Entity. Our healing is entirely up to us.

If you suspect you have a deal with an Opportunistic Entity, and you want to be released from the contract, you will have to not just have the extraction done, but you will have to change your life dramatically. First, the original contract with its benefit to you personally has to be looked at. Then you'll have to ask yourself whether you want to give up the mindset that keeps the contract in place. Because if you don't change your life, the Entity or one just like it will return to take its place. The shaman can extract again and again, but it is the Empath and the Entity who make the deal between them. The shaman doesn't break the deal, the Empath does.

However, if you are willing to change your life, step out of the Victim Stance, and be vigilant about falling back into any Victim Role behavior or mindset, extracting an Entity is straightforward. The Entity might retaliate briefly in an attempt to scare you into vulnerability again, such as one Entity who shook a client's bedside table after an extraction in an attempt to scare her back into vulnerability, but the Entity can't reattach without some sort of agreement in place. So in that way, we need not fear more attachments if we do our work and step back into personal power and personal responsibility.

If you suspect you have one of these attachments and are willing to do the work, now is the time. Given how fast human consciousness is shifting right now, it's a great time to change your life and release yourself from these old ways of being. Once you have finished your work, if you have children of your own, it's probably a good idea to have them checked for Opportunistic Entities as well. Parents who have an Entity attached unconsciously set up an environment that makes it likely that the young children in the home will also be vulnerable. Empath parents, when they don't have Opportunistic Entities attached, tend have good energetic radar. If you have an Entity, assume your radar is not working properly until you have completely your own personal work.

5 GENERATIONAL IMPRINTS

When I work with my clients long term, I have my clients get to know their patterns intimately. The reason for this is so that they can gain enough consciousness to change at least one little action in the pattern the next time it arises. Each change little by little leads to a dismantling of the pattern. Catching ourselves before we can take the actions that lead to the unhappy outcome becomes a practice. It's a difficult, confusing practice because our intuition and our instincts are inaccurate when it comes to navigating the pattern—otherwise we would have mastered it long ago and we wouldn't need to consult a shaman. Deliberately questioning our instincts when we've worked especially hard to accept our intuitive side can be highly confusing.

When the pattern is triggered and running our lives, all our decisions are driven by the pattern, but it feels like our decisions are driven by our intuition and our higher instincts. We are sure we are absolutely right and justified, when instead we are just living out the same old mistake again. This is why each of us must get to know our patterns and how we tend to project those onto our relationships when we are NOT triggered. The place to start when we notice a pattern (an outcome that has repeated three times) is to ask ourselves when we first experienced the pattern or felt the feelings in the pattern. Usually it stems from early wounds in childhood—many times because of a misunderstanding or a trauma inflicted by one of our parents, intentionally or not. Many times these traumas are handed down generation after generation, so that energetically, emotionally, and mentally they carry the extra force of our lineage.

GENERATIONAL IMPRINT PROJECTED ONTO OTHER RELATIONSHIPS

As an example, one of my clients had worked hard on a mother issue that manifested as her giving her power away to other women she thought of as peers. Somehow the relationship would turn from one of peers to one with her in the one-down position as either lowly apprentice or mentee. The outcome of this pattern was that she rejected the woman who put her in the one down position while feeling betrayed and embarrassed. To prevent this pattern from manifesting the same outcome of suffering and a broken relationship, we had to look at where it came from.

This client had a withholding, selfish mother. As a consequence my client consciously and unconsciously sought approval but was usually shot down by her mother. Without knowing it my client put these other woman peers in the mother-position. Usually what would happen is that she would ask for advice in an area especially dear to her heart, expecting to be treated as a peer. But the advice hardly ever felt like it came from a peer. Somehow the other woman wound up in a more powerful position than my client and abused that power. Part of this is vibrational, (after all, she unconsciously came to these relationships as a supplicant for her mother's approval), but we also looked at how my client asked for and received the advice.

She had to assume that she was going to set the situation up unconsciously to unfold so that the other woman would belittle her. While an important and essential part of healing this pattern was to work directly with her own relationship with her mother with soul retrieval and underworld work, my client had to carefully look at how she operated within peer relationships with other women at the literal level as well. With these deeply ingrained patterns, ones that we've been living out for several decades, we have a sort of body-memory that we must overcome. We must also look at what we do, think, and feel as the pattern unfolds.

My client had to assume that when she felt betrayed, annoyed and confused the pattern was in play and that she wasn't seeing the other woman clearly. Walking away from the relationship was the last step in the pattern. Did she really want that outcome this time or could it be avoided? Much of the time the pattern came about because she asked for advice as a peer, but the advice came back with her in the one down position. She had to look at how she asked for advice. What language did she use? Was her subtext one of supplicant asking for a favor? Was she inviting a shift from peer to mentee? Changing her language so that she remained in a strong peer position also helped.

One aspect of the mother-daughter relationship that my client didn't see without outside help from her shaman was that her mother had her own insecurities that she projected onto her daughter. Because these patterns have a strong energetic component, my client's pattern meant that unconsciously my client would pick a peer that was likely to project her insecurities onto my client and then put my client down, just like her mother did. To be on the receiving end of this would be no fun for anyone, so it wasn't a big surprise that my client ultimately walked away from these relationships. However, before she walked away she spent considerable time wondering if she had imagined the abuse of power when everything had begun so nicely.

However, walking away without consciousness around the pattern only set up the next iteration to manifest in the same way. Unconsciously my client was looking for perfect advice from a perfect mother-substitute, but was doomed to disappointment because no one can give perfect advice and no one can be a perfect mother. The rejection of her mother took place through other women but wasn't a resolution because the original wounds and unconscious beliefs weren't healed. Doing the soul retrieval and underworld work helped to heal those wounds and beliefs, but now she had to work on taking different actions when the pattern unwound itself again.

The same feelings and thoughts arose when the pattern came up again, but the difference that next time was that my client could say to herself, "This is the pattern. I'm in a peer relationship with a woman that I really like. At some point I'm going to set this up so that she'll project her insecurities on to me, and then I'll have reason to reject her. I'm going to be aware for each of these stages." As my client practices she catches herself at the last stage and can avoid rejecting the friend but sets better boundaries about asking for advice. In the following iteration she catches herself feeling those feelings of betrayal but notices in time that in a peer relationship she can take advice or leave advice, but she shouldn't shoot the messenger and so manages to not act on those hurt feelings. In a later iteration she might catch herself asking for advice but then notice that she herself has set herself up as a mentee instead of a peer. In a later iteration she might notice that she's picking insecure women to be peers with even though they might be highly qualified in their fields. She might then choose not to get too close to them or she might not be completely taken by surprise when those women project those fears and insecurities outward. Each iteration of the pattern is an opportunity to master the pattern until finally it is broken and my client has taken her power back. She's also managed to grow up a part of herself that still needed approval from her mother.

Sometimes we have experiences with soul retrieval and underworld work that are so spectacular that the energy work session clears everything up on the emotional, mental, and literal levels. I love those. But, with an unhappy pattern that's become well ingrained by taking action again and again in the literal world, it usually takes several practice attempts at the pattern to fully unwind it. Staying conscious, giving ourselves a break for having to practice at it, and making those small changes again and again means that we heal our lives and give ourselves freedom.

GENERATIONAL IMPRINT SHIFTING TO THE NEXT GENERATION

Generational imprints or family curses can mean that we repeat the same behaviors that lead to unhappy relationships between generations, or that we set up the same physical illness generation to generation. How to we break these curses? The good news is that shamanic energy work can be highly effective in helping to break a family curse. The other good news is that generational imprints can be positive and life affirming—such as the ability to make money, good health, or an appetite to learn new things—can also be passed down the generational line.

Previously I spoke of a mother-daughter imprint that my client projected outward onto her other relationships with women. Such relationships were particularly painful, but my client was doing great work on getting a handle on the projection. She was particularly concerned about this family curse because she wanted to have a daughter. She didn't want to pass on the curse to her daughter in which her daughter would experience her as selfish and withholding. My client was conscious of the possibility and afraid of unintentionally passing on this imprint; she understood the strength of generational imprints having worked on hers. She knew ahead of time that she was likely to repeat a similar outcome with her own daughter.

This client has a much better chance than most of not passing on a family curse because she makes the assumption right away that she could (unintentionally) manifest such a horrible outcome. It takes a very brave and conscious person to realize that she is capable of acting in the same hurtful way that her mother had done to her. These curses tend to easily pass generation to generation because the Victimized party stays in the Victim position and cannot consider that they could ever be in the Bully position with the next generation. My client automatically assumed that she would play out her role as mother in the curse if she did not stay conscious. In that way she took a step back from the pattern so she could begin healing it.

However, most of my clients are not this self-aware. I had another client ensnared in a mother-daughter family curse. In this case my client was focused on how hurtful her mother was, and on how she wanted their relationship to be different. My client was firmly in the Victim position, but not only that, she wasn't willing to give up this position until her mother changed into the mother she wanted. In effect, my client was not only staying Victim, she was refusing to grow up; she was giving away her power to her mother instead of focusing on healing herself.

The complication here was that this client had a little girl. Because the family curse had not been healed within my client, it was a given that my client was already setting up her relationship with her daughter so her daughter would bear the curse. My client certainly did not intend to do this, but because her energy was focused on herself and her own pain, she could not step back enough to see how she was creating the same relationship with her own child.

What was interesting here was that people close to her could already see the curse unfolding, but my client was blind to it, just as her mother was blind to it. This client had a hard time doing what my previous client had done—she could not assume that she was very likely and fully capable of hurtful, neglectful, and selfish behavior toward her daughter. Part of this was the strength of the generational imprint, but some of this was denying the hard reality of being an effective parent. Effective parenting means sometimes setting aside our own needs to meet the needs of our child. The child can't meet her own needs—that is the parents' job. One cannot be an effective parent if we stay in the Victim position or the Child role. The Victim and the Child have no power—that power is outside in the hands of others. With her energy focused on how wronged she had been by her own mother, and how angry and hurt she was, she did not see that that was distracted from and resentful of her child's own needs.

Many times what is most striking about a family curse is how it unfolds without the people inside the curse being aware of how their thoughts and actions are making it unfold. The people involved may desperately set the intention to not repeat the curse, but they do anyway. These curses have that type of strength to them. Even though the energy work will help, once again, in this case it will take effort and practice for this client to make sure she cleans up her part of the curse so that it won't impact her daughter.

The most effective way for my client to do this is to understand how the curse for her family works without placing herself in any role. In other words, what does the mother do in this curse? In this case the mother is so distracted and focused on herself that she ignores her daughter pleas for attention and connection and actively resents her daughter's having needs. The daughter focuses on her pain and how if she could only get her needs met and get the attention of mother then all would be well. The key for my client is to take herself out of daughter position, which she understand extremely well, and put herself into the mother position, which is the bad guy or the Bully position. The Bully position is always the hardest one for us to see in ourselves. Of course my client does not want to see herself in the mother position of this curse because the mother is the one who inflicts the damage.

Then the next step is to assume that she will unconsciously do everything and anything to act out the role of mother as defined by the curse. She will ignore her daughter's attempts at connection, and she will actively resent her daughter and her needs. The key is for my client to realize that this is a given—this is how the curse plays out—it has nothing to do with her personally as a good or bad person. In this case the curse contains ironic elements—it is only because my client is focused on her mother that she ignores her daughter and sets up the same relationship, creating a vicious cycle from generation to generation. Each generation feels screwed by the one before it but screws the one after it all the while thinking of themselves as loving mothers. My client isn't generating this unhappy outcome because she's a bad person or a bad parent—she's generating it because she is not taking responsibility for it.

The other side of breaking the curse is giving up the daughter role as well. She has to let her mother off the hook by growing up and not needing approval, connection, or permission from mother. Of course this is excruciatingly difficult, partly because of the nature of the curse, but for this client a lot of it is the inability to accept the way things are for her mother. This client will never ever get that relationship with her mother, ever. The longer she believes she might, the longer she wastes energy, and the more likely she will not be able to curb her tendency to play out the mother position of this curse. Many of you will object that of course the possibility exists that her mother will grow up and change like my client could. Yes, that is a possibility, but hanging on to that possibility from the Child Role and the Victim stance is never helpful and in fact squashes the probability of that outcome. Allowing that possibility from an Adult stance off the Drama Triangle makes the possibility more likely for all involved. The key is to give up attachment to having the ideal, imaginary, fantasy relationship with her mother. It simply does not exist.

In giving up the daughter position she has to give up asking for attention and connection with her mother. She has to give up nursing her pain and being angry. In other words, she has to deal with her personal wounds without a hope of any change with her mother. She has to be willing to heal herself, to take full responsibility for her child self, grow that child self up with nurturing that comes directly from inner self. All of this type of healing work can be furthered along with soul retrieval and underworld work. She has to meet her own emotional needs and give up expecting mother to finally come through. Then she'll know how to nurture her own daughter.

If my client can heal herself and meet her needs by growing herself up from within, she will likely break this curse. This particular curse depends on her staying a child, staying Victim. It also depends on her being the distracted, resentful mother. Any time my client feels resentful toward her daughter she has to assume the curse is in play. Any time she feels angry with her mother, she has to assume she's fallen back into the Victim role. As you can imagine, this is hard work, staying this conscious, calling herself on her hard thoughts and emotions. But if my client plays neither resentful mother nor angry daughter, she's stopped the momentum enough that she can choose to respond differently to her daughter. My client has a chance to stop a horrible outcome that has been tormenting her family for generations. She should think of it as her sacred mission of this lifetime.

What makes these curses so difficult is how hard it is for the person within the curse to see the pattern, and how she plays BOTH roles in the pattern once it passes to the next generation. If you know you have a family curse, please take it to a shaman. The shaman can unravel the original bind on that energetic level, but your shaman will also help you map out the curse on the mythic level to help you be aware of how it plays out in your life. Then it is up to you to do the hard work on the symbolic and literal levels of not letting it pass down to your children. Take it as a sacred mission—if you break the family curse, then you have saved generations of your family from suffering.

6 THE DOUBLE BIND

One of the most difficult situations to help a client heal is unraveling a double bind. This is because the bind is usually invisible to the client, but leaves her feeling paralyzed and frustrated with herself. No matter what action the client takes, she loses.

UNRAVELLING A DOUBLE BIND BY GIVING UP A FAULTY FAMILY BELIEF

I had a client recently who could not manage to keep her house clean. Although she had been a lawyer, and thus had to have some organizational skills to be successful, she could not organize her home. My client was an Empath with a highly sensitive nervous system. Empaths become upset when exposed to too much clutter. My client lived in a state of frustration with herself and agitation from the disorganization.

None of the usual coaching work we did together solved the problem. No matter what plan she put into action, the clutter became worse and worse. Finally, we began searching for double binds. A double bind is a lose-lose situation. A telltale symptom of the double bind is paralysis. The goal of the shamanic work is to turn at least one part of the bind, preferably both, into a win situation. But before we do that, the bind must be discovered.

A great way to gain insight into this type of bind is to look from the Mythic Level using pictures and fairy-tale telling. My client wrote a mythic story based on the images within the three cards she pulled from her favorite oracle card deck. As we reread her story, I was able to spot her double bind. One of the most important emotional things she craved was to be loved and accepted by her family. And yet, her experience with her family was that when she was herself, she was ridiculed and devalued. Her subconscious belief was that if she acted just as herself for herself that her family would not love her. The double bind was that she had to be loved by her family, but her family would reject her if she pursued her art. However, she couldn't be personally happy unless she pursued her art.

My client had quit her law career in order to focus on a more creative lifestyle. Her soul's longing was to be a writer and an artist. But, once she had the freedom to concentrate on her art, she felt constantly blocked. The clutter started to build soon after. The clutter was actually a form of self-sabotage—it made her feel so anxious she literally had no energy to put into writing or art. If she cleaned up her house and became organized, she would have no energy drains, at least on the physical plane, and so would have the space and energy to pursue her art. So, the clutter served as a defense mechanism so she wouldn't risk losing her place of belonging within her family. It also hid the true cause of her anxiety—losing her family's love. This was a great "ah ha" moment for her.

Once my client became aware of the unverbalized rules or belief system of her family, she was able to see how she was playing into the flawed family belief system and reinforcing it by making certain choices. The norm within her family was to put the security of the family ahead of the individual desires of family members. While this may have been necessary a few hundred years before when concentration on physical survival was all that life was about, that was no longer the case for her generation, but a part of her was unconsciously choosing to live as if it were so. The price for each family member in holding to the family rule was a feeling of dissatisfaction, misdirected anger and resentment, and a sense of lost youth and dreams.

My client's true nature was full of fun, vitality, and passionate energy. Living by the family rules literally meant rejecting her nature. Her new awareness meant that her vibration shifted as well so she was able to start taking different action. We also did energy work to clear up the family contracts she held around belonging and toeing the line for survival's sake. She made the commitment to herself, that even if she lost the relationships with her family and they rejected her forever, she wanted freedom to pursue her Soul's calling. The price of breaking away from the belief system did mean her relationships with her family were strained. However, now she was able to make a conscious choice to pay that price. It was with this change in consciousness both in the under and middle worlds that set up the change within her so she could change her life.

UNRAVELLING A DOUBLE BIND BY SHIFTING PERSPECTIVE

Sometimes the dismantling of a double bind happens with a shift in perspective. I had a client who was in such a severe bind at work that he was unable to make enough money to support his family. He understood the importance of changing his belief system, but nothing seemed to budge the bind.

His bind was around holding to his personal integrity. If he made money in his job selling vacation packages, then he'd feel like he compromised his integrity. But if he didn't make money in his job, then his family would suffer. In some cases, he loved selling to people. They wanted a great vacation, and he could provide it for them. In other cases, he was reluctant to sell because he believed they couldn't afford it or that they really didn't want the package. He did not want to act in any way unethically.

What I noticed was that even when ordered by his boss to tell outright lies, he refused to do so. Eventually a new boss who had ethical standards replaced the old boss. The only remaining problem was that my client couldn't sell to people that he knew could not afford it at the moment. What I found interesting was that when those people scheduled an appointment with him, he wasn't working that day. My interpretation was that Spirit was helping him protect his integrity.

Since Spirit was running interference for him so well, and since an odd set of coincidences had led him to this job, we made the assumption that this was where he was supposed to be at the Literal and Symbolic Levels. Next we shifted from viewing his situation from the Symbolic Level to the Mythic Level or Soul' Journey perspective.

From the Soul's Journey perspective, my client's purpose was all about being in service to Spirit. Everything about this man's life was guided from Spirit. As such, he was someone that Spirit could use for good works. I asked him to consider making the assumption that he was where he was supposed to be, and he was there to be of Service.

He needed to consider that from his limited perspective, he could not tell how his prospective customer would use a vacation for their Soul's Journey. Perhaps for this person even a vacation they appeared to not be able to afford was a lesson in the importance of priority. Perhaps this vacation would save a marriage or conceive a child. Perhaps this vacation would lead to the relaxation that would in turn activate the spark of someone's creativity, and the world would enjoy a new Harry Potter series. We just couldn't know or predict from the state of our ordinary minds.

He also needed to consider that he could not make the decision for the client whether to buy a package or not. That was his client's decision. As such he was overstepping a boundary and in a sense usurping his client's power, a horrifying insight. As long as he acted ethically by presenting all the facts of the cost of the package, including the obligations and limitations, he was doing his job with integrity. This shift into a wider perspective was very heartening for my client. But, there was something else that wasn't allowing him to let go and let himself do his job.

We moved to energy work. My client blew that reluctance into my stones and we began a soul retrieval session. I saw that in a past life he had given up his life in exchange for holding up his principles. He had been part of a firing squad that was asked to shoot innocents, and instead of shooting he got into the firing line himself. But he left behind a family.

I believe what had happened was that the danger and the fear of compromising his ethics in his sales job had triggered the old imprint of this past life, setting up a very powerful bind for him. He literally would rather die than compromise his ethics. In other words, the price of holding to his ethics was not just his life but his ability to provide for his family as well. His being asked to compromise his ethics at his sales job triggered the emotional trauma from the past life. As a consequence he was finding it hard to be of financial support to his family—he was reenacting the outcome of the past life. By honoring and witnessing this past life, and by working with

THE EMPATH AND SHAMANIC ENERGY WORK

the past life aspect of him to release him in this lifetime, my client could feel the shift within him. He got to keep all the gifts from the past life including some pretty stellar karma for the integrity he held in his previous life. But with the healing, the grief and the tragedy could be witnessed, and then that energy could dissipate.

The double bind (he must support his family, but if he does he'd compromise himself. He'd rather die than compromise his integrity) was no longer an issue. Now he can move forward understanding that he is a conduit for joy and happiness in his selling of vacation packages, and that Spirit is going to work well with him because of his ethics. His ethics are not in his way in this lifetime; in fact they are a distinct advantage. Part of that is the faith to understand that when he sells a vacation package that that vacation is serving a larger picture and has bigger meaning than he can know.

7 SELF-SORCERY AND THE INTERNAL BULLY

Many of my clients have suffered terrible abuse as children. Soul Retrieval work is instrumental in clearing out these past experiences and returning energy and consciousness to the client that left because of the trauma. These people are truly victims, and the Shaman steps in as a real rescuer to do the Extraction and Soul Retrieval work that they cannot do themselves. However, when the victim begins to feel her power and strength, leaving the lifelong Role of Victim can be so scary that she chooses to go backwards, sometimes with Self Sorcery. The client, most of the time unconsciously, becomes frightened that she might not handle stepping out of the Victim role well, so she Bullies herself instead.

When we've suffered terrible abuse, we've learned how to be a Victim. We've also learned how to be a Bully, too, because we've had such a perfect example. Remember, the Bully has all the power over the Victim. When a lifelong Victim is encouraged to step into Power, subconsciously she believes she is being asked to step into the Bully role since that is how she has experienced power. Understandably, stepping into her power can be frightening. Staying a Victim is much safer than exploring power.

The Victim has internalized not just the roles, the actions, and the cues, but also the energy of each position on the Drama Triangle. Both the Victim and the Bully exist within the self (and the Rescuer as well.) If we tap into an archetypal trigger for one of these roles, it becomes too easy to unconsciously step into whatever role is required at the time. The hardest role for any person to see within themselves, especially one who has been severely abused, is the Bully.

Even without an external Bully, the Victim can tap into her own internal Bully vibe to the point that inexplicable things start to happen such as headaches, the cat acting strangely, and the kids becoming recalcitrant. The acting out of the Internal Bully is actually a common self-sabotage for all of us, but if we were abused as children, our Internal Bully can be quite intense. The Internal Bully is also the inner-critic. It's the voice that leads many Empaths into chronic depression and suicidal tendencies. These Victims have been so used to being abused that they can tend to think it is right and proper to resort to self-abuse. Unfortunately, the tendency to self-abuse always leads to abusing others. Most Victims believe they reserve the abuse just for themselves; they can be horrified to be told that of course they are spreading the abuse and its negative, heavy vibration to their spouses, children, and friends as well.

I had a client who had been severely abused by her mother emotionally and physically. She had broken off contact with her mother and most of her siblings, who were still stuck in a destructive and crazy family system. We did incredible underworld work together. My client was slowly stepping out of the Victim role and taking on more and more personal power and responsibility for her life. Right before one huge shift in empowerment, she began to feel like her mother had hired a sorcerer and was attacking her. She thought she might be crazy, because she described her mother as a fundamentalist fanatic—the last thing her mother would do would be to hire a sorcerer. The "attacks" escalated with her children acting out. Even her cat started having inexplicable physical symptoms. However, when I tracked what was going on, I could find no evidence of her mother or a sorcerer.

Instead what I saw was the Internal Bully keeping her in place so she wouldn't be empowered. My client felt more secure and comfortable tapping into the Bully vibration so she could firmly be in a Victim position from which she would need a Rescue from me. Of course, if there were a sorcerer involved, this would be a legitimate Victim/Rescuer situation. This client, being highly introspective and observant, suspected that she was creating the weird symptoms in herself and in her cat.

She feared that if she admitted to the self-sorcery that I would call her crazy and not want to work with her as a client. But actually, her awareness and the incident itself was an indication that we were making progress together. This would not have come up if her internal boundaries were not being stretched into a more healthy state. The minute she realized what she was creating, the cat's symptoms miraculously disappeared.

Pointing the progress out to her was a revelation, but an even bigger one was pointing out how much power she literally did hold. She was able to make herself and the cat sick, not to mention scare herself half to death. The psyche is very complex; these shadow parts we hold can carry power over us instead of for us.

For my clients of severe abuse, the long-term goal to health and empowerment is to incorporate and integrate the shadow of the Bully. By holding them safe and using baby steps, together we look at how these life-long Victims actually do have within them Power held by their internal Bully. True personal power comes with knowing that they have the capacity within themselves to be completely evil and yet they choose not to behave that way, especially toward themselves.

Usually it is a revelation for them to hear me tell them, "You know, I know I'm completely capable of being a sorcerer, being an abuser, being evil/bad, etc. I'm not in denial about holding both the good and the evil within me. That acceptance lets me be at choice about it. That is why I'm not going to act that out in the world." And once they are able to do that, they claim all the power of the Bully without acting out the Bully. It's a process, but it's the path to wholeness.

Part of the challenge for lifelong Victims of severe abuse is that the Victim role is well known, and that it has the perk of the Victim never having to be responsible for the self. Someone else takes over that role instead. The Victim may be disempowered, but at least being a Victim is well known and therefore safe, even if Life is limited and unenjoyable.

Empowerment requires all of the human condition being held and acknowledged and owned. This process is frightening. It is much safer to hold that internal Bully outside of the self instead. Having the safe container to explore these disowned aspects of the self is essential to the integration of those parts. Exploring slowly, with role-playing, with baby steps, is crucial. My client is making amazing strides in allowing herself to interact more with the world, and have more of an effect on it. She no longer needs the role of Victim to feel comfortable and safe.

For the rest of us, it's an interesting exercise to look at where we'd rather be Victim than take on full responsibility for ourselves. Where is it easier to be powerless but safe? Where do we claim life just happened to us and ignore the choices we've made? Where do we invite Bullies so we won't have to take an original or scary step? Where do we attack and Bully ourselves? Where do we try to Rescue instead of put our energy into something more creative? The more we get off the Drama Triangle of disempowerment, the more we step into power, and the more we are able to be co-creators with Spirit.

8 THE POWER OF STORY

Stepping out of the Victim Role requires draining the power of our Victim Story. As we've seen earlier, the vibration of Victim is so powerful that it can pull in a Bully in the external world to make sure that we stay Bullied. We also have seen that lifelong Victims stepping into personal empowerment can step into a Bully role instead, since the only examples they have seen of Power are from Bullies. These Victims can perform self-sabotage, or in the case of my client in the previous essay, self-sorcery, to make sure they do not step into Power.

Once we understand both these concepts, we can set aside those times when we do play the Victim and attract Bullies, and we can also set aside those times when we are so afraid of stepping into power that we self-sabotage instead. We can remind ourselves that we have the ability to change these situations by changing our internal state. But what we might overlook is that we're investing our power in our stories around being a Victim.

Being a Victim is an archetypal role. That means that when we are in that state we call in information not just from our own personal story that happened literally to us, but also information from the collective. We may overlook the power of the collective story of Victim and become trapped in trying to discover what our literal story was. For people who have been victims of abuse to the point where they have blanks in their memories, much confusion can arise when we try to determine what actually happened to us.

While there can be healing in researching what actually happened to us, I have found that too much research into the details can turn into a trap. This trap develops when a Story is built around being a Victim, and that Story gains more and more power. We may have a feeling that leads to a repressed memory, and then we may hypothesize about what literally happened to us. We build up a belief system based on our story. We can have memories surface that are ours, and we can also have glimpses of suffering from the Collective that are not ours. This adds strength to our Story. If we are Empaths, this is very likely to happen. Sorting out these different "memories" can be horribly confusing, and it can lead to an endless search for the reason and meaning behind these memories as if each memory literally happened to us.

As Empaths we take our emotions and our feelings very seriously. Also, Empaths have active mental minds, so building a structure to explain our emotional state is easy for us to do. What we do not realize is that we are identifying with the story—the story becomes who we are. We become more and more invested in our story, even though in the present moment we could tell ourselves a completely new, empowering, hopeful, happy story and have that be just as true as the old story. We've given our energy, our life force, to maintaining this old, wounded, victim story. Soon, the story begins to feel like it has a life of its own, and we can feel like Victims of its power as well.

I had a client who had a tragic story that involved being raped as a preteen. She had turned this story into an identity through most of her life. She told herself (and select others) that she was a rape victim and that she would probably never get over it. Telling herself this story generated feelings of hopelessness and powerlessness within her. In other words, she rewounded herself every time she told this story! Once the people closest to her knew the story and accepted her (and it), the story faded into the background. However, unresolved wounds always surface at one point or another—it is an opportunity to heal the wound and move on. Unsurprisingly, with each boyfriend she met, the Story would resurface in order to be healed.

Unconsciously my client's system wanted to be rid of the energy of this story and the original wound. Each new boyfriend meant an opportunity for the closeness and intimacy to help move the stuck energy out of her system. Her stress and worry over becoming sexually intimate with her new boyfriend triggered the repressed feelings. The part of her that wanted to heal wanted someone to witness the wounding and trauma she had went through. During intimate moments, the old overpowering feelings of being trapped and sexualized resurfaced within her. She would panic during sex. None of her boyfriends knew what to do with her fright, becoming frightened themselves. So she would bury the Story and the feelings. Her panic reactions would then cease until the next relationship.

My client could feel the Victim energy just waiting to pop itself out again. What was also confusing was that in the literal world she was adding to this Story with each attempt at trying to understand it and explain it. However, any addition to the Story did not help to resolve the original wound. She was drawn again and again to the wound, but tried to heal herself from the place of Story. Her friends and boyfriends had all told her that something terrible must have happened to her for her to have the physical reactions she was having. Unwittingly each well-meaning friend and boyfriend added more investment for her into maintaining her Victim story. She had been hanging on to these explanations of her emotional state for so long, that they felt like the truth.

Many times these kind of memories and the accompanying feelings that come with them come from the birth experience, especially if the birth was stressful. Each birth can have a sexual component to it for the person being born. Feelings of being trapped, suffocated, or simply being frightened to death mixed in with sexual feelings at a time when we cannot have a memory based on words means that there is danger later in finding a story to fit these old memories and feelings. I suspect that my client had tapped into something like this, either from her own birth, or from the collective, when she confessed with deep shame and embarrassment that she suspected her Story was not literally true.

If it were not true, then that would mean she had made it all up, and then what sort of horrible, crazy person would do that? So, with that judgment hanging over her head, the Story had to be true or else she was a crazy person. But how could it not be true with the physical reactions she was having during sex? She wasn't making those up. But if her Story were literally true, then she had to be screwed up anyway. She didn't want to be a mess for the rest of her life. She was in a terrible double bind of being a damaged person either way—either a victim of rape or a victim of believing her own storytelling and getting others to believe it as well.

I told my client to stop caring if the Story were literally true or not. From the Shaman's perspective, it is a Story, and we are not our stories. At the same time Story has incredible power over us, so she needed to heal the stuck emotions around the Story and drop it. The Story might as well be true even if it were entirely fictional, because her whole system behaved as if it were true! Once my client decided it didn't matter what the Story was, only the force behind it mattered, she let herself off the hook for being crazy. Then she could explore without judgment how best to allow her healing to unfold. She followed where these memories and feelings were coming from with her new husband using tantric techniques.

What they discovered together was that she recounted the Story a little differently each time she remembered it. The details in the form of flashes of memory kept changing. Not everything she remembered could have happened to her. (These were probably glimpses of other Stories or memories from the Collective.) In fact, as she and her boyfriend allowed the story and the memories associated with it to unfold with no judgment on their part, the details of the story became more violent and more grotesque. It was almost as if the Story made a last ditch effort to stay powerful and keep my client (and her boyfriend) hooked into her old Victim stance. Somehow, in the witnessing, in the non-judging, and in the deciding that it didn't matter if it were true or not the Story began to lose power. It drained away because, I believe, she no longer was holding on to this Story as an Identity. It was simply something to observe.

I believe she had the immense physical reactions she had because the energy of this Story was stuck in her second chakra. She had grown her story so much by feeding it the old feelings in telling the story that the story had an energetic imprint within that life force chakra, which also controls sexuality. The chakras connect not just to the energetic level, but to the mythic where the Collective is, and to the emotional and physical level, too. When my client and her boyfriend used sex to clear out the Story, they cleared out the imprint within her second chakra on all four levels of reality. The story was so gone that she completely forgot about it until years later she sent me a new a client who was having problems sorting out memories of abuse from her past. I actually had to remind my former client that she had gone through something similar years before.

When we tap into an archetypal role we can pull in all sorts of information from the experience stored in the Collective Mind. It is important to be very careful choosing what Stories we tell about ourselves and others so we don't amplify our personal story into a Collective Story. Perhaps it is more important to give up Story all together once in a while to remind ourselves that we are not our Stories, too.

One way to heal a Story that we aren't sure is personal but could be Archetypal is to assume that it is Archetypal. That way, we understand that by doing our personal work with the Story we are healing some aspect of the Collective, too. This makes our healing work not just about us personally, but also about being of service to all of humanity. As Empaths we can easily channel Archetypal stories and make them into personal stories. We must be sure to give ourselves empowering Stories!

9 DEATH AS ALLY—SHEDDING RELATIONSHIPS

Many of my clients who work with me are committed to following a conscious spiritual path. As such they are bringing awareness to all aspects of their lives, including their relationships. With this new awareness, they may decide that they want to change these relationships. Many times the other person within the relationship is not interested in changing and wants the old way back. Sometimes this transition can be made easier if the person who is growing in awareness understands the other person's point of view.

I had a client who had been single up into his early thirties. Paul had a large, close-knit group of college friends he saw on a regular basis, even though many of them had to travel across country to maintain their annual tradition of group gatherings. Paul, because he had been single for so long, was able to go to every gathering and be the social glue for his group. But, what he really wanted was a soul mate of his own. Most of his friends were married. He also wanted marriage and children, and he wanted to move on with his life.

Paul did considerable personal work to heal what was blocking him from creating a soul mate relationship. He healed wounds that stemmed from failed relationships within his family of origin, so he could step into a relationship that really satisfied him. However, one consequence that stemmed from these wounds was that Paul clung to his friends in a way that many people cling to family relationships. He had created a role within his family of friends to be the glue holding the group together. Paul tended to instigate these gatherings, plus Paul's personality made others feel comfortable and welcome. Paul put considerable time and effort into maintaining these relationships. To make space for that new mate, he had to loosen his ties to his group.

Soon after he did his healing work, he attracted his ideal mate into his life. He was the happiest he had ever been. Both his family and his friends welcomed his new mate into both groups. However, as this couple established itself tension between the couple and the friends grew, especially when it became apparent that Paul would no longer be available as the social glue for the group. Like most people who make a new relationship the central focus of their lives, he didn't call his friends as often because he spent most of his free time with his fiancée. One friend told Paul that even though he was getting married, that didn't mean he should change.

This, of course, is a ridiculous statement to make to a man that is about to marry. Of course marriage brings tremendous change to the individual, and the change is wanted. What the friend could not express was that he felt threatened by the inexorable change that a wife would bring to the friendship and the group interaction. He was resisting the loss he would feel at forever being placed on the back burner in terms of priority. This man, even though he was thirty years old and married himself, regressed back to his teen years in which he hadn't learned how to deal with these inevitable changes gracefully.

Most human beings resist change, especially change that we do not invite ourselves. With help, Paul was able to see from the soul's journey perspective what his friend was going through, even though at the same time he was horrified that his friend was acting in such a juvenile manner. Paul attempted to help his friend adjust to the change by reassuring his friend that there would always be room in his new life, even though it wouldn't be the same amount of room. He understood that although his upcoming marriage was triggering the behavior, it wasn't entirely personal.

Unfortunately, the friend reacted badly to the reassurances from my client and blamed my client's fiancée for the rift in the friendship. Although he attended the wedding, after the wedding he ignored invitations to come visit or to get to know Paul's wife better. He also ignored for several months requests to talk about the change within the friendship. While Paul had held that soul's journey perspective for his friend, the withdrawal was still very hurtful. It was because of the withdrawal and the willingness to inflict hurt in that fashion that

Paul decided that he no longer wanted the friendship, especially since his friend had chosen to blame his new wife for the change. Paul concluded that it was unacceptable for his wife to endure the bad vibes from his old friend, no matter the length of the friendship.

At Paul's birthday more than a year later, his old friend called to wish him happy birthday, and expected to pick up the friendship as if nothing had happened. Paul had moved on to form other friendships within his new life, and was no longer interested in the old friendship, and yet felt guilt for not being interested. His friend had decided to adjust to the changes in the relationship, but unfortunately it was too late. What was ironic was that the old friend managed to create his worst fear: losing his friend to marriage. Of course, he did not lose the friend to marriage; he lost his friend by his own failure to deal with his own fears and reactions to this change.

Many of my clients feel torn when a former friend or family member wants to reestablish a relationship, but they are no longer as interested. The other person in the relationship had taken hurtful actions, intentionally and/or unintentionally, but has not apologized or made amends. My client may understand what was triggered in their friend, and may unconditionally love them and remember fondly the old relationship. However, in many cases, my client has moved on in the time it takes that old friend to adjust. Or, it can be as simple as not wanting to be too close to someone who is likely to react negatively rather than examine behavior that could be hurtful. These clients tend to feel like they are unforgiving or even unspiritual that they cannot manage to reestablish the relationship.

It is perfectly OK to say no to a relationship, even one that has a long history. It is perfectly OK to cultivate relationships with others that are simply easier and more rewarding. At the same time, it is also a healthy choice to establish new relationships with these old friends and family members, but with different boundaries and ways of relating if that is wanted and possible from both sides. There is no wrong answer to choosing to have the relationship or not. It is more a matter of what we each want in our lives. We get to decide what is best for us separate of any other judgments from the outside. And sometimes, some relationships must die in order for new relationships to come in.

Paul wasn't being cruel or unforgiving to his old friend. But he did understand that the friendship didn't have room for him to be a fully-fledged adult with a marriage that took precedence over his group of college buddies. Paul took the time to communicate with his friend to help him adjust, but when that didn't happen, he was prepared to go his own way. Although this was a loss, it was necessary so Paul could have room to establish a new group of friends in which his wife would be included. Paul still has a great group of friends, but they are not the same group of friends. Paul changed, but his old group wasn't willing to change with him.

This is a very common occurrence, and while the loss should be mourned, it shouldn't hold us back from establishing the relationships we really want in our lives. It is natural for us, especially when we do our personal work, to outgrow the people around us. Relationships that can grow with us are wonderfully rewarding, but many times that doesn't happen. It's important to let those relationships go and honor them when it's clear they need to die, and continue to move forward to what really sustains us.

10 HEALING SEVERE ABUSE

Most of us begin the Spiritual Search in order to find happiness, enlightenment, and more joy in our lives. Our lives aren't working the way we would like, we want more from Life, and so the healing journey begins. In many spiritual circles right now, there is much focus on the positive, on what is working, on ease and grace, on flow of good energy and on being in right relationship with all things, and mostly on being a successful, happy, spiritually good person. And, those goals usually do come for the true seeker.

However, what is not acknowledged is that the path toward healing can be very painful, uncomfortable, confusing, and downright difficult. When these difficulties arise, we can become disillusioned and concerned that we are doing something wrong, when in fact we are right on track. We can worry about our thoughts not being positive when much of the time they are obsessive, negative, and even mean. We can worry that our emotional state is not of one of happiness and relaxation when in fact it may also be at the same time anxious, fearful, angry, and even hateful.

We have been taught by the popular spiritual manifestation gurus that having pleasant thoughts and feeling good are essential to creating the life we want. This is true, but it is also true that in order to heal, we must bring up and out all the old thoughts and emotions, patterns and imprints that have prevented us from creating what we wanted in the first place. If we believe that we must be positive and happy to create the lives we want, we can end up repressing even more those internal places that need witnessing and healing. As long as those places within us are repressed, unacknowledged, and unwanted, they hold power over our lives. These places become hidden from us, unavailable to us. As long as we are defining them as negative, we are keeping ourselves from considerable resources both emotionally and energetically.

I have much respect for the clients who work with me because they are committed to jumping into the morass of their hidden selves. They have had glimpses of the hidden because it is reflecting back to them unwanted experiences. They learn how they are creating their part in the dramas of their life. Bringing this energy to consciousness is very painful, alarming, and in some cases humiliating. But, it is part of the process. These imprints within us literally create our reality. By becoming conscious of how they create our external circumstances, we can change them internally and create the external circumstances that we would like instead.

Some of us aren't that wounded, and so just learning that our thoughts and emotions are creative sets us on our way with being conservative and focused with our thoughts, words, and emotions, and we begin manifesting what we want. But for the rest of us who have suffered deep woundings, those patterns themselves have power, and they contribute to creating our external circumstances for us. Changing those patterns can be a very confusing process, because they literally do create our external reality through projection.

I am working with a brave, beautifully creative but blocked client right now. She has suffered tremendous abuse within her original family, mostly from her mother. This pattern is so ingrained within her that her vibration attracts to her on the outside women, mostly neighbors, who verbally abuse her and her children, but then these women expect her to stand there and take the abuse. Eventually she has enough of it and she and her family move to a new neighborhood where the pattern repeats itself.

Until my client heals the pattern inside of herself, it will literally repeat its creation in the external world. That is how much power my client has that is not within her conscious control. Bringing it into her conscious control is an amazingly confusing process. First, she has to understand intellectually what the pattern is. Luckily for my client she saw herself as the common denominator in every move to a new neighborhood and understood there had to be something about herself that was creating the situation.

This allowed her to look carefully at the pattern she had with her mother, and to see how she was repeating the mother pattern in the rest of her life. In the original incident with her mother, she took horrible abuse both physically and emotionally for years, tried to please by doing what was expected of her, and then finally became angry enough to cut her mother off. For my client she began to see that it was her own vibration of passive victim that was pulled out of her neighbors unreasonable bullies. The passivity she learned from her original family made her stand there and take the abuse instead of walk away from it. The pattern played itself out by my client having enough abuse, concluding her neighbors were crazy people, and then her running away by moving.

Once my client understood the pattern, she began to shift it with changes in behavior, and with the energy work, (illuminations, extractions, soul retrieval, and death work) to remove the heavy energy from her system. She became lighter and lighter, more conscious of what was going on around her, and more detached and observant of herself and the behavior of others. The pattern was still there, but she had it under control.

She reached the point where she was feeling free, ready to go out into the world and create, and she was amazed at her level of energy and how good she was feeling. It is right at this point where it is very common for progress to seem to go backward instead of forward. One reason this happens is that we are each part of a system within our family, our jobs, and our community of friends, and the system can resist the changes in the individuals. In her case, her son, who was used to having his mother hovering around him, began engaging in dangerous behavior to get her attention back from her own creative endeavors.

It wasn't that her son was trying to thwart her; it was that he was uncomfortable with the change in his mother's energy. All of us like the status quo to some extent; changing it can be a scary transition. I encouraged her to believe in her son's strength and give him more responsibility to help her around the house to help him change his own role within the family from a young boy needing to be over protected to a young boy ready to engage his world responsibly.

As the pattern that is up to be healed begins to pass through our system, our system digests it on the physical, emotional, mythic, and energetic bodies. So, as we heal we have the new system in place while the old system is leaving, which usually makes the average person who doesn't know the healing process feel like he or she is going insane. In my client's case, her imprint popped back up to the point that she felt compelled to act it out again.

We had just had a session in which I reiterated that there was no point in moving again until she healed the internal imprint around her mother, or else she would just take it along to the new neighborhood. She saw that this was true, but the urge to move was very strong. She also had the pattern of trusting women and then having them abuse her and her trust. I was now put in the position where the trust we had built between us was under attack from the imprint. Now she didn't feel like she could trust me and wanted to cut me out of her life. To my client's credit, she paid for three sessions in advance to make sure she didn't do so.

And she rode out the intense feelings. She knew intellectually that I was holding space for her and was there as healer. She allowed herself to feel her deep distrust toward me. All her internal patterns came up in the form of some pretty startling projections. She was convinced that I was a rigid fundamentalist Christian ready to persecute her and her children. Of course, this was so far off the mark that it was easy for her to own the projection.

As she owned it and stuck with it, she broke out in a rash. Her physical body was trying to let go of the deep patterning in this way. All the emotions were at the surface—her emotional body was also letting go of the deep wounds she had suffered. I encouraged her to put all of these emotions into a sandpainting which allowed the imprint to process on the Mythic plane, giving the emotional and physical bodies a break from the deep work. I also did a huge clearing of her chakras, a death rites process, to clear out the imprint that was triggered and playing out.

Then the symptoms subsided, and she was back to moving forward again to the next layer of the imprint: how her husband was affected. In fact she had been moving forward the whole time, but had been in a precarious position of believing the reality the imprint had created and of acting on it just as she was about to burn it off. I have deep respect for clients who stick through this process and come out the other side. They then know that they can do this again with the next imprint, or even with another layer of the same imprint. They become willing to deal with their patterns as they come up, and while this is still a challenging process, they are on their way toward mastery and freedom.

While my client still has considerable work ahead of her to mulch those imprints into the dirt and reclaim her power, she has moved something huge for herself, and already many many blessings have entered her life because she made room for them. My teachers at the Four Winds call this relishing death—allowing what needs to die to die so that the new can come in. My client is well on her way to creating a new life for herself and her family.

Mastery doesn't necessarily mean we feel good, happy, and enthusiastic all the time. What it means in the healing work is that we can hold our big, expansive selves at the same time we allow our little selves their existence, too, trusting the process to heal those deep imprints. Oddly enough, when we are willing to hold it all, it becomes easier to create the lives want.

11 CONCLUSION

Although many of these examples deal with extreme cases of abuse, shamanic energy work can help break less severe patterns. Shamanic Energy Work makes a good complement to traditional therapy. In fact, many of my clients see a therapist and receive body work while doing shamanic work with me. If you have a pattern you have tried to break, but it still shows up in your life, consider taking it to a shaman. Next in this series of eBooks we'll delve into closer detail on the Empath as Archetype, what motivates us, and what patterns we tend to run up against.

12 RESOURCES

Here's a short list of my favorite books that got me started on my path:

Shamanism and Healing Work:
Shaman Healer Sage by Alberto Villoldo
Mending the Past Healing the Future with Soul Retrieval by Alberto Villoldo
The Reluctant Shaman by Kay Cordell Whitaker
Soul Retrieval by Sandra Ingerman

Intuition, the Chakra System and Psychic Development:
The Psychic Pathway by Sonia Choquette
True Balance by Sonia Choquette

Personal Transformation and Manifestation:
Your Heart's Desire by Sonia Choquette
Finding Your North Star by Martha Beck
Steering by Starlight by Martha Beck

The Spiritual Enneagram:
Personality Types by Don Richard Riso with Russ Hudson
Wisdom of the Enneagram by Don Riso and Russ Hudson

Creativity:
The Artist's Way by Julia Cameron
Vein of Gold by Julia Cameron

The following are teachers and schools that I highly recommend:

Sonia Choquette offers trainings and workshops for developing intuition.
Marv Harwood of Kimmapii Spirit Energies is the shaman I go to for graduate training
The Four Winds Society trains students to be shaman healers
Wake and Kinlen Wheeler of Sacred Pathways offer training and shaman gatherings

Contact Information:

If you would like to contact me, please visit my website at www.elainelajoie.com My website has many free resources and essays for Empaths, plus a list of practicing shaman I highly recommend.

Much love to you,

Elaine

ABOUT THE AUTHOR

Elaine La Joie is a shaman and certified life coach. She has been in private practice since 2002 helping Empaths heal old traumas and patterns so that they can create the lives and relationships that they really want.

Before Elaine opened her practice she worked at the University of Texas Austin in the psychology department and at the Oregon Medical Laser Center as a researcher. Elaine holds degrees in physics and applied physics. She realized a few years into this career path that she was jealous of the other researchers who loved their careers. This, plus a psychic opening led her in a completely new and unexpected direction.

Not wanting to advertise as a psychic, Elaine went into Life Coaching instead. She trained with Coach For Life, became certified, and then was horrified when all her clients started asking for readings or training. After a few more years of resistance Elaine trained with the Four Winds Society and later with Marv Harwood of Alberta Canada.

Elaine maintains a limited private practice so she can concentrate on writing. She lives in Oregon with her family.

CPSIA information can be obtained
at www.ICGtesting.com
Printed in the USA
LVHW012246010419
612618LV00038B/1103/P